CRIME AND DETECTION

DEATH ROW AND CAPITAL PUNISHMENT

Crime and Detection series

- Criminal Terminology
- Cyber Crime
- Daily Prison Life
- Death Row and Capital Punishment
- Domestic Crime
- Famous Prisons
- Famous Trials
- Forensic Science
- Government Intelligence Agencies
- Hate Crimes
- The History and Methods of Torture
- The History of Punishment
- International Terrorism
- Major Unsolved Crimes
- Organized Crime
- Protecting Yourself Against Criminals
- Race and Crime
- Serial Murders
- The United States Justice System
- The War Against Drugs

CRIME AND DETECTION

DEATH ROW AND CAPITAL PUNISHMENT

MICHAEL KERRIGAN

MASON CREST PUBLISHERS
www.masoncrest.com

Mason Crest Publishers Inc.
370 Reed Road
Broomall, PA 19008
(866) MCP-BOOK (toll free)
www.masoncrest.com

First printing

1 2 3 4 5 6 7 8 9 10

Library of Congress Cataloging-in-Publication Data on file at the Library of Congress

ISBN 1-59084-375-4

Editorial and design by
Amber Books Ltd.
Bradley's Close
74–77 White Lion Street
London N1 9PF
www.amberbooks.co.uk

Project Editor: Michael Spilling
Design: Floyd Sayers
Picture Research: Natasha Jones

Printed and bound in Malaysia

Picture credits
AKG London: 18, 20, 34; Amber Books: 47; Encompass Graphics: 46; Mary Evans Picture Library: 8, 10, 12, 13, 14, 17, 19, 23, 26, 27, 29, 30, 32, 58; Popperfoto: 21, 24, 39, 42, 48, 50, 66, 71, 72, 73, 81, 84, 87; Topham Picturepoint: 6, 35, 37, 38, 40, 41, 44, 49, 51, 53, 54, 56, 57, 60, 61, 63, 64, 68, 74, 76, 77, 79, 80, 83, 86, 89.
Front cover: Corbis (main and center right), Topham Picturepoint (center left), Popperfoto (bottom).

CONTENTS

Introduction

From the moment in the Book of Genesis when Cain's envy of his brother Abel erupted into violence, crime has been an inescapable feature of human life. Every society ever known has had its own sense of how things ought to be, its deeply held views on how men and women should behave. Yet in every age there have been individuals ready to break these rules for their own advantage: they must be resisted if the community is to thrive.

This exciting and vividly illustrated new series sets out the history of crime and detection from the earliest times to the present day, from the empires of the ancient world to the towns and cities of the 21st century. From the commandments of the great religions to the theories of modern psychologists, it considers changing attitudes toward offenders and their actions. Contemporary crime is examined in its many different forms: everything from racial hatred to industrial espionage, from serial murder to drug trafficking, from international terrorism to domestic violence.

The series looks, too, at the work of those men and women entrusted with the task of overseeing and maintaining the law, from judges and court officials to police officers and other law enforcement agents. The tools and techniques at their disposal are described and vividly illustrated, and the ethical issues they face concisely and clearly explained.

All in all, the *Crime and Detection* series provides a comprehensive and accessible account of crime and detection, in theory and in practice, past and present.

CHARLIE FULLER

Executive Director, International Association of Undercover Officers

Left: For and against, feelings about capital punishment run high, with agreement only that the question goes straight to the heart of what America stands for. Here a member of the Catholic peace campaign protests outside the state capitol building in Atlanta, Georgia.

The Death Sentence

Capital punishment is surrounded with solemnity, for no graver penalty could be exacted than that of death, the extinguishing of an individual's existence. Not that it has always been this way. For much of human history, a life could depend upon the whim of a king; while in 18th-century England, a man could be hanged for the theft of a sheep.

Looking at the history of the death penalty, and the countless different ways in which it has been used, suggests there is far more to it than simply ending a life. What one civilization sees as a public deterrent, another regards as a private business between the criminal and the law. In some cultures, protracted pain has been part of the punishment; in others, pain has been avoided at all costs. Some societies have used different methods of execution for people of different ranks.

There is far more to the story of the death penalty then first meets the eye. Derived from the Latin word, *caput*, meaning "head," the term "capital punishment" is used mostly on symbolic grounds, the head being regarded as the seat of life and consciousness in the human body. Today, capital punishment as it is exercised in the United States is unmistakably the product of a modern age in terms of both the high-tech methods that are involved and the elaborate legal and psychological safeguards governing its use. At the same time, however, capital punishment has a history that has been many centuries in the making. The purpose of this book is to achieve a better understanding of both.

Left: Reputedly a powerful wizard, and certainly a forceful influence on the feelings of the masses, Pituanius was viewed with profound suspicion by the authorities in imperial Rome. Finally, in A.D. 30, the Emperor Tiberius declared him an enemy of the state, and he was hurled to his death from the top of the Tarpeian Rock.

IN THEORY

For as long as human civilization has existed, so, too, has the death penalty. Yet some caution has to be exercised in saying this because it is difficult to tell when the tradition of a socially ordered judicial execution separated off from that of human sacrifice aimed at appeasing an irritable deity. Around 1775 B.C., the ruler of Babylon, Hammurabi, laid down the first known system of law. Known as the Code of Hammurabi, it included capital

The Greek philosopher Aristotle turns his back on his beloved Athens, having outraged the authorities by his outspoken opinions: had he remained, he would have found himself facing the death penalty.

THE FATE OF TRAITORS AND MURDERERS IN ANCIENT ROME

In the early days of ancient Rome, traitors were hurled from the "Tarpeian Rock" located just outside the city. A rough and ready sort of justice, it was more elaborate than it sounds. The fall, although high enough to break bones and damage internal organs, was not generally sufficient to kill the person outright. So the victim lay incapacitated at the bottom, unable to move, dying over several days from exposure, hunger, and thirst. Murderers, on the other hand, were tied in sacks and thrown into lakes or rivers to drown.

punishment for a number of crimes.

There has often been a divide between the attitudes of **intellectuals** to capital punishment and those of society as a whole; this was evident as long ago as classical Athens. The philosopher Aristotle felt that the satisfaction of the one dealing out the punishment or the well-being of the public could not alone justify any punishment. The purpose of any penalty must be the improvement of the offender's character, yet this could hardly be possible if the punishment was death. Aristotle himself would have to leave Athens for a lengthy **exile** under the shadow of the death penalty, having fallen foul of those in charge of the ancient city.

Athenian statesmen showed little sign of being influenced by arguments against the death penalty. A generation previously, in fact, in 399 B.C., the father of all the philosophers, Socrates, had been compelled to commit suicide by drinking hemlock, on the grounds that his teachings "corrupted youth." Athens was the world's first **democracy**, and Socrates, as a free citizen of Athens, had the right to commit suicide, which was considered to

Surrounded by his distraught supporters, Socrates takes the poisonous cup of hemlock that will take his life, establishing a long tradition of suspicion between intellectuals and ruling elites in Western societies.

be a relatively dignified death. Just as he was entitled to vote in elections, the free citizen was allowed to take his own life if found guilty of a crime. Slaves, however, had no such privileges. If found guilty, they were simply beaten to death.

Among the ever practical, down-to-earth Romans, there is little sign of any serious debate. For grave crimes, especially murder, death was the accepted penalty. In the "12 Tables" of the law, the murder of any freeborn Roman was considered equivalent to parricide (the murder of one's father), making it a symbolic offense against authority and the state.

The Romans' concern with reputation and public image is also reflected by the fact that one could be executed for bearing false witness against—or even for singing a satirical song about—a fellow citizen.

The first Christian martyr, Stephen, is stoned to death by an angry crowd: today, he is revered as a saint. The specter of lynch law has haunted the entire history of capital punishment, with modern governments going to great lengths to ensure that justice is truly done.

VICTIMS' JUSTICE

Like Christians, Muslims share the scriptures of the Old Testament with the Jews, although these texts are seen through the filter of the subsequent teachings of the Prophet Muhammad and other thinkers. The great sacred book of Islam, the Koran, contains the thoughts of God or Allah as dictated to the Prophet by an angel, and offers a view of punishment that is similar to Biblical tradition. "The free for the free, the slave for the slave, the female for the female," says the famous text, but many scholars insist that this does not mean "a life for a life." The principle, they say, is payment, not punishment; restitution, not revenge. The offender has to do everything in his power to make up for his wrong. So, while allowing the death penalty for various crimes, including murder, *shariya* law has never seen execution as its first preference. For example, the families of murder victims have always been urged to accept financial compensation instead. It is assumed that the decision should rest with them, however, rather than with the court. As the sufferers in the case, it is for their benefit that justice is administered.

THE BIBLICAL AND THE BUDDHIST

The Hebrew scriptures, on which the whole Western Judeo-Christian tradition is founded, provided a confusing guide to future legislation. Although the Fifth Commandment warned: "Thou shall not kill," the Biblical Old Testament also ordained the death penalty for many civil and religious crimes. This included everything from murder to eating while ritually unclean.

The "new covenant" represented by the Gospels placed far greater emphasis on forgiveness and restraint, although, significantly, some have said, Christ never explicitly calls for the dismantling of the old legal system or the ending of the death penalty. His intervention in the case of the woman taken in adultery (John 8), where he says, "He that is without sin among you, let him first cast a stone at her," stops short of suggesting that the victim does not deserve to die. This ambiguity was only underlined by the pronouncement of St. Paul in his Epistle to the Romans (12, 19): "Vengeance is mine, I will repay, saith the Lord." Should "Vengeance is mine" be taken to mean, "I bring vengeance; I stand for severity of punishment, so you should treat your criminals harshly on my behalf"? Or, on the contrary, did it tell humanity: "Vengeance is mine, not yours, so you should leave punishment to me"? The dispute would continue well into the modern period.

Further east, in India and beyond, great religions, like Hinduism and Buddhism, find themselves in a similar double bind, committed to the sanctity of life, but aware of the need for society to be governed in peace and order. Many Hindus who refuse to eat meat on ethical grounds still believe that capital punishment has its place in a system of justice.

There are others who strongly disagree with this point of view. The dilemma facing Buddhists is more extreme, since the Buddha whose teachings they follow was more uncompromising in his views. The strict Buddhist would—quite literally—never hurt a fly. The reality seems to be, however, that the more impossibly strict the religious prohibition, the easier it is to ignore. Regimes in Buddhist Myanmar (formerly Burma) and Thailand have shown no qualms about applying the death penalty, although capital punishment in these countries has little to do with religious practice.

IN PRACTICE

From the earliest times, the death penalty has been applied in an enormous variety of ways. The Egyptians are believed to have impaled wrongdoers on wooden stakes and left them to die in the desert sun. This was not only agonizing, but also public, an essential element in many forms of execution to set a warning example to others. This practice was widely used throughout the Middle East and it grew in sophistication into the method of crucifixion eventually adopted by the Romans. The Gospel accounts of Christ's crucifixion are the best record we have of this terrible punishment. The cause of death was not generally by loss of blood or the trauma of having spikes driven through the feet and hands. Death was usually caused by suffocation due to the crushing pressure on the lungs by the overstretched shoulders and chest muscles.

In medieval Europe, the favored method of capital punishment was hanging. The prisoner dangled from a rope, sometimes for several hours, and slowly strangled. Once again, there was an element of public display in the punishment, the victim's body often left hanging long after death.

HUNG, DRAWN, AND QUARTERED

For some especially hideous crimes, one death alone was not believed to represent adequate punishment, so authorities began the practice of "hanging, drawing, and quartering." Having been brought close to death by hanging, the victim was taken down, his stomach slit open, his internal organs "drawn" forth from his abdomen, and held up before his horrified eyes. If he survived this terrible ordeal (and a skillful executioner could make sure he did), he would then be "quartered": his body divided into

The most famous execution of all, shown here in a 15th-century illustration: Jesus Christ is crucified between two thieves. At the foot of the cross, his mother Mary faints from intense grief while, unconcerned, a pair of soldiers play dice over who should have the victims' clothes.

Guy Fawkes and his friends, the Catholic conspirators who had attempted to blow up the English Parliament in the "Gunpowder Plot" of 1605, are dragged through the streets of London on lengths of fencing.

four. Treason, a crime against the king, was seen as a threefold offense, against the king himself, against God, whose representative he was, and against the country. This was the symbolism underlying a punishment that amounted to three executions in one: death by strangulation, death by disembowelment, and death by mutilation.

OFF WITH HIS HEAD

Beheading has been a favored form of the death penalty in several civilizations. A quick and comparatively neat method of execution, it was

Executed by King James I in 1618 for going beyond his orders as naval commander, Sir Walter Raleigh maintained to the end the self-confident courage that had made him so devastatingly effective—and so dangerously wayward—as a military leader.

BREAKING ON THE WHEEL

A particularly brutal method of execution, used as recently as the 18th century in parts of Europe, was known as "breaking on the wheel." This was every bit as crude and cruel as it sounds. The unfortunate prisoner was splayed out across a wheel or X-shaped frame and tied firmly down, and then his limbs were broken in turn with blows from a sledgehammer. He would then be allowed to lie in agony for some hours before the executioner finished him off with a smashing blow to the stomach or chest.

for a long time reserved as a privilege for those well-born individuals who had offended their ruler. This was the case with the English explorer Sir Walter Raleigh, killed on the orders of King James I in 1618. Feeling the edge of his executioner's axe, he is famous for commenting: "This is a sharp medicine, but it is a sure cure for all diseases." He then scornfully rejected the offer of a blindfold, saying "Think you I fear the shadow of the axe, when I fear not the axe itself?"

LET THIS BE A WARNING TO OTHERS

Anecdotes such as the story of Walter Raleigh hint at an important aspect of capital punishment. Throughout history, it tended to be a type of public performance, with a theater all its own. This trend reached its height in 18th-century England, when under the terms of the notorious "**Bloody**

A thief is publicly beheaded in the China of 1904, his grisly end intended as a warning to those watching. The risk with this sort of ceremony is that, however solemn it may be in theory, it ends up degenerating into a vulgar spectacle that trivializes justice.

Code," more than 200 offenses, from shoplifting to sheep stealing, carried the death penalty. Prisoners were paraded through the streets of London to the execution place at Tyburn to warn other **miscreants** what they might expect if they persisted in their criminal ways. So commonplace were these processions, however, that, far from impressing the urban poor with their solemnity, they became festive occasions of the most wild and raucous kind, known as the "hanging fair." And rather than setting terrifying examples, the condemned became swaggering heroes. Often, indeed, that state's authority was undermined because the public felt that the punishment was undeserved or, at the very least, too harsh.

The **satirical** poet Jonathan Swift captured the prevailing mood to perfection:

> *As clever Tom Clinch, while the Rabble was bawling,*
> *Rode stately through Holbourn to die in his calling;*
> *He stopt at the George for a Bottle of Sack,*
> *And promis'd to pay for it when he'd come back.*

Not everyone saw the amusing side: a less buoyantly satirical writer than Swift, the serious-minded novelist Samuel Richardson was appalled at the behavior of the crowd around the scaffold:

"At the place of execution, the scene grew still more shocking; and the clergyman who attended was more the subject of ridicule than of their serious attention. The psalm was sung amidst the curses and quarrelling of hundreds of the most abandon'd and profligate of mankind: upon whom (so stupid are they to any sense of decency) all the preparation of the unhappy wretches seems to serve only for the subject of a barbarous kind of mirth, altogether inconsistent with humanity."

Such drunken carnivals could hardly be said to have any sort of deterrent effect. Thus, through the 19th century, executions were increasingly carried out behind closed doors.

REVOLUTIONARY JUSTICE

The guillotine has become the unmistakable symbol of the "Reign of Terror" that followed the French Revolution of 1789, when the king, queen, and thousands of their aristocratic supporters were publicly executed. This does something of an injustice to Ignace Guillotin. He had not invented the machine, but he had perfected it and campaigned for its use for humanitarian reasons. The task of developing a quicker and more painless means of administering capital punishment concerns lawgivers even today, and the contribution Guillotin made was by no means negligible. The idea that the act of beheading might be mechanized was not new. In fact, similar devices had been in use in parts of Europe since medieval times. However, with its triangular blade, the guillotine was by far the quickest, cleanest, and most efficient form of execution.

An American Tradition

The principles of "liberty, equality, and fraternity" fared badly in the French Revolution, which soon broke down into a ruthless "Reign of Terror," but freedom and democracy were having a better time of it across the Atlantic. There, since 1796, the American settlers had been fighting to throw off the rule of their English colonial masters and building a republic in which there might be (in Abraham Lincoln's later phrase) "government of the people, by the people, and for the people." One of the first challenges facing those who built our nation was that of deciding whether, when, and in what manner the death penalty should be applied: humanitarianism was an important principle of the new republic. Yet so, too, was that of justice, the need for each individual's freedom to be balanced with those of his or her fellow citizens, and the central democratic duty of upholding the rule of law.

THE AMERICAN DEBATE

Capital punishment is not mentioned in the U.S. Constitution of 1787. However, this does not mean that it is "unconstitutional." Rather, the Founding Fathers seem to have taken the use of the death penalty for granted. The Fifth Amendment assumes that the death penalty exists, as does legislation passed by the first Congress. Yet there were signs of some discomfort with a system substantially inherited from an English one that was associated with the oppression of the American colonies and notorious for the excesses of the "Bloody Code." George Washington's friend and revolutionary inspiration, the French soldier the Marquis de Lafayette,

Left: A portrait of Benjamin Franklin, who believed that, far from discouraging violence, the death penalty effectively promoted it, giving citizens a sense that the life of the individual was held in low regard by their society.

launched his own eloquent plea against its use. He was opposed to the imposition of the death penalty, he said, and expected to remain so until he could be convinced of "the **infallibility** of man." Others, such as Benjamin Rush, Benjamin Franklin, and the Attorney General William Bradford, opposed the death penalty on the grounds that it had a brutalizing effect on society as a whole. By sending out the message that the state did not hold human life in high esteem, it tended to encourage, rather than minimize, violent crime, they said.

Thomas Jefferson seems to have sympathized, up to a point, at least. As governor of Virginia (1779–1781) and then again as president of the United States (1801–1809), he worked vigorously to reduce the number of crimes for which the death penalty could be applied. Despite this, Jefferson did not want to do away with the death penalty altogether. He may have objected to what he saw as the sheer bloodthirstiness of existing laws; at the same time, he insisted on society's "right to erase from the roll of its

The French general Marquis de Lafayette held a simple case against the death penalty. In his belief, it made the possible miscarriage of justice irreversible: what amends could be made to a man or woman who had been incorrectly executed?

Like the rest of the Founding Fathers, Thomas Jefferson had his reservations about capital punishment, but believed the ultimate sanction, for the benefit of society, was needed to help prevent the gravest crimes.

CRUEL AND UNUSUAL?

The Eighth Amendment of the Bill of Rights seems absolutely clear in its prohibition of any "cruel and unusual punishment," until one asks just what would define such a punishment. The fact is that one man's "cruel and unusual punishment" is another's justifiable punishment "to fit the crime." It is ironic to reflect that the wording of the American Bill of Rights was taken just about word-for-word from its English equivalent of 1689, a document that had done nothing to prevent the introduction of the 18th century's "Bloody Code."

members any one who rendered his own existence inconsistent with theirs; to withdraw from him the protection of their laws, and to remove him from among them by exile, or even by death if necessary."

Yet this ultimate measure would only actually be called for, Jefferson was convinced, "for murder and perhaps for treason." Other crimes were best punished "by working on high roads, rivers...etc, a certain time proportioned to the offense." Under his influence, while capital punishment continued to be used in the United States, it was on nothing like the scale sanctioned by English conventions of the day.

THE EUROPEAN VIEW

The French Revolution may have collapsed into carnage, but the mood that first inspired it still lived: a boundless confidence in the capacities, and in the essential goodness, of humankind. Stirred by Englishman Sir Isaac Newton's reordering of the scientific universe, a new generation of progressive thinkers in France, called *philosophes*, had, throughout the 18th century, been celebrating the limitless potential of humankind for progress. At the same time, they were proclaiming the birth of the "Age of Reason,"

French officials oversee the guillotining of three rebels in an African colony in 1900. In the 19th century, European powers established versions of their own systems in their colonies: many of these countries maintained these traditions even after independence.

CAPTURE OF JOHN BROWN.

A pivotal moment in the Civil War—and, arguably, in the moral history of modern America—was the capture of John Brown at Harper's Ferry. Brown's dignity in meeting death boosted not only his antislavery cause, but also the concern that such executions were out of place in a civilized society.

urging their readers to turn their backs on every sort of superstition and barbarity: capital punishment, they firmly believed, was both. It also granted the monarch what now seemed an outrageous power over another's life and death. The impact of such thinking was felt throughout the 19th century in just about every corner of the world.

Earlier in history, in 1764, Italian writer Cesare Bonesa Beccaria had written a work entitled *Essay on Crimes and Punishments*, which proved profoundly influential. "The punishment of death is pernicious to society," writes Beccaria, "from the example of barbarity it affords. If the passions, or the necessity of war, have taught men to shed the blood of their fellow creatures, the laws, which are intended to moderate the ferocity of mankind, should not increase it by examples of barbarity, the more horrible as this punishment is usually attended with formal pageantry. Is it not absurd, that the laws, which detest and punish homicide, should, in order to prevent murder, publicly commit murder themselves? What must men think, when they see wise magistrates and grave ministers of justice, with indifference and tranquility, dragging a criminal to death, and whilst a wretch trembles with agony, expecting the fatal stroke, the judge, who has condemned him, with the coldest insensibility, and perhaps with no small gratification from the exertion of his authority, quits his tribunal, to enjoy the comforts and pleasures of life? They will say, 'Ah! Those cruel formalities of justice are a cloak to tyranny, they are a secret language, a solemn veil, intended to conceal the sword by which we are sacrificed to the insatiable idol of despotism. Murder, which they would represent to us a horrible crime, we see practiced by them without repugnance or remorse."

AN AMERICAN HANGING

"John Brown was hung today," wrote Commander Thomas J. "Stonewall" Jackson from Charlestown, West Virginia, on December 2, 1859, his Confederate forces having captured the famous soldier and antislavery campaigner. Jackson wrote: "He behaved with unflinching firmness. Brown had his arms tied behind him, and ascended the scaffold with apparent cheerfulness. After reaching the top of the platform, he shook hands with several who were standing around him. The sheriff placed the rope around his neck, then threw a white cap over his head and asked him if he wished a signal when all should be ready—to which he replied that it made no difference, provided he was not kept waiting too long.

"In this condition he stood on the trap door, which was supported on one side by hinges, and on the other by rope, for about 10 minutes, when Col. S. told the Sheriff 'All is ready.' A single blow cut the rope, and Brown fell

John Brown's body might molder in its grave, but, said the song, his truth went marching on, an inspiration to the Union forces in the Civil War. Politically motivated executions often rebound on those who carry them out, making the martyr into a focus for the political passions of a people as a whole.

AN ANOMALY ADDRESSED

The Gregg Ruling of 1976 dealt with the difficulty highlighted most famously by Benjamin Franklin: that laws that are "too severe" are "seldom executed." The introduction of "bifurcated trials," with two separate hearings (one to establish guilt or innocence, then another to decide upon the sentence) helped to deal with the age-old problem of juries' reluctance to convict where they thought a death penalty might follow.

through about 25 inches, so as to bring his knees on a level with the position occupied by his feet before the rope was cut. With the fall, his arms below the elbow flew up, hands clenched, and his arms gradually fell by spasmodic motions—there was very little motion of his person for several minutes, after which the wind blew his lifeless body to and fro—

"I was much impressed with the thought that before me stood a man, in the full vigor of health, who must in a few minutes be in eternity."

THE CONTROVERSY CONTINUES

The pressure for **abolition** was always there, in 1845 finding a voice in the American Society for the Abolition of Capital Punishment. In 1892, New York representative Newton Curtis brought forward a bill for the complete abolition of capital punishment at a federal level. His bid failed, but prompted a modest revival in the fortunes of the anti-capital punishment movement. In 1897, Congress passed "An Act to Reduce the Cases in Which the Death Penalty May be Inflicted," which did just that, in particular, making the death sentence a matter of the judge's discretion at trial, rather than **mandatory** in every case.

By 1917, 10 states had abolished the death penalty for all crimes, with the exception of treason, yet it would be wrong to assume that abolitionism

THE HISTORY

Pennsylvania was the first state to conduct executions within the walls of its prisons in 1834. With its influential Quaker community, Pennsylvania pioneered penal reform, but other states abolished public executions in the course of the 19th century. In 1846, Michigan did away with the death penalty for all crimes except treason; a few years later, Rhode Island and Wisconsin abolished it altogether. However, more than 100 years after Pennsylvania made executions private, Kentucky was still holding executions in front of large crowds.

The states that maintained the tradition of hanging did try to make it more humane, increasingly using the "long drop." Previously, a prisoner had been "turned off" a ladder, platform, or the back of a cart and left to dangle, "dancing" in the air. Now, the neck was noosed with a longer rope and the body placed over an abruptly opening trapdoor, so that the force of the fall snapped the neck, making death instantaneous.

On July 7, 1865, George Atzerodt, David Herold, Lewis Paine, and Mary Surratt go to their deaths together at Washington's Old Penitentiary. They had conspired with John Wilkes Booth to assassinate Abraham Lincoln: Booth himself was shot dead in the course of his apprehension.

was making slow yet steady progress. In fact, as the temperature of the debate heated up through the early decades of the 20th century, public opinion swung violently back and forth, polarized by a series of sensational and highly controversial cases.

On the one hand, there were the Chicago "Thrill Killers," Richard Loeb and Nathan Leopold, Jr., wealthy white students who, in 1924, kidnapped and killed a 14-year-old boy. They were given what many people felt were wholly inadequate life sentences for a crime apparently committed simply for the excitement of it. On the other hand, there were Nicola Sacco and Bartolomeo Vanzetti, two Italian anarchists—revolutionaries dedicated to the total overthrow of government—who were executed in 1927 for a murder committed in the course of an armed robbery aimed at raising funds for their cause. There seems, in truth, to have been good forensic grounds for finding them guilty, but there was also undoubtedly an atmosphere of hysteria in the media at the time. Some ill-advised remarks of the judge, moreover, left many with the feeling that Sacco and Vanzetti had been tried for their political beliefs and not their actions.

ABOLISHED AND REINSTATED

The arguments continued through the decades that followed, the abolitionist case gaining the most ground, assisted to some extent by tensions between the federal and state systems. A number of high-profile court cases had important implications for the status of capital punishment in the United States. The Supreme Court's decision in the case of *Trop v. Dulles* (1958) had no direct bearing on the death penalty, yet campaigners seized on the judgment that the Eighth Amendment involved an "evolving standard of decency that marked the progress of a maturing society." This was interpreted as meaning that times changed and so did acceptable standards, leaving the way clear for a challenge to the death penalty.

What had been appropriate to the early 19th century might be deemed "cruel and unusual punishment" now. Whatever might be the case in legal

The merest hint of a "political" execution makes its victim into a potent symbol of state oppression. Sacco and Vanzetti were guilty of the crime for which they were tried, but their names still became a rallying point for radicals mobilizing support for left-wing causes.

theory, the death penalty did seem to be becoming less acceptable in legal practice, especially if the number of actual executions was anything to go by. While there had been 1,289 executions in the United States in the

This famous photograph, taken with a concealed camera strapped to the ankle of a *New York Daily News* reporter, shows the execution of wealthy wife Ruth Snyder for the murder of her husband in 1928.

Apparently in a grave but philosophical mood, California killer Caryl Chessman sits to be photographed at San Quentin, just 48 hours before the time appointed for his execution in the prison's gas chamber in February 1960.

"Crimes of the 20th Century," reads the title of the book: some feel strongly that execution is a state-sanctioned crime, the U.S. government in the end being no better than the murderers it has put to death in the name of justice.

1940s, the figure dropped to 715 in the 1950s; it fell away to 195 for the 1960s. A national opinion poll in 1966 showed only 42 percent of Americans supporting capital punishment: the practice seemed to be withering away of its own accord. In 1972, it seemed, the death penalty had finally received its own deathblow with the landmark Supreme Court case of *Furman v. Georgia.* In its judgment, the court effectively suspended the death penalty in those 38 states that still exercised it, ruling that under existing statutes, capital punishment did indeed constitute "cruel and unusual punishment."

The Supreme Court's objection to the death penalty as applied in Georgia and elsewhere was that, in allowing individual juries to decide when it should be applied, it opened the way to sentencing that was arbitrary and inconsistent and, therefore, unjust. In 1976, however, the state of Georgia was back before the Supreme Court with a proposal that judges guide juries to their decisions along consistent guidelines. This was approved, and the death penalty was reinstated. With its implicit acceptance that there was nothing unconstitutional about capital punishment *in principle*, the "Gregg Ruling" opened the way for other states to rewrite their statutes, too.

It has an almost medieval air of clanky obsolescence today, which makes it hard to recall that, on its introduction 100 years ago, the electric chair appeared to be the last word in modern punishment: efficient, clean, high-tech, and—above all—humane.

The Death Penalty in Practice

Capital punishment in the United States is performed only under strictly limited conditions. In fact, in some states, it is not used at all. Very few categories of crime carry the death penalty—very few categories of murder, even; only the most dreadful offenses are punished in this way.

In the course of 2001, there were only 66 executions in the United States as a whole. The intensity of the controversy generated may give a misleading impression of the scale of the phenomenon. It is right that this should be so. The society that takes life lightly or casually can hardly lay any claim to the status of civilization. However, it is important, too, that we retain our sense of proportion. Every U.S. state is aware of its awesome responsibilities in what is literally a matter of life and death, and enormous efforts have been made to ensure that the system is humane.

For historical reasons, the methods of execution employed may vary a good deal from state to state, but common to all is a scrupulous care that unnecessary suffering is not caused. The law may call for the giving up of a life, but it emphatically does not allow for physical or mental torture: the authorities go to great lengths to ensure that this should not occur. That the state should seem to lean over backwards to protect the rights of the man or woman responsible for some especially heinous murder may be a cause

Left: Protestors parade behind a replica electric chair outside the U.S. embassy in Madrid, the Spanish capital. Nothing divides America and Europe more starkly than their respective attitudes to capital punishment.

William Mason, a Death Row prisoner at the Ellis 1 Unit, near Huntsville, Texas, works on the details of an appeal against his conviction for murdering his wife. Like many other inmates, Mason devotes hours each day to his legal researches.

of public exasperation, and private anguish for their victims' families. In the end, though, the meticulous observance of even the vilest murderer's rights is our guarantee that we remain a just society.

THE WHERE, WHY, AND WHO

Of the 50 American states, 38 have the death penalty; the 12 exceptions are Alaska, Hawaii, Iowa, Maine, Massachusetts, Michigan, Minnesota, North Dakota, Rhode Island, Vermont, West Virginia, and Wisconsin. A survey conducted by *The New York Times* in 2000 found that, on average, these states had lower homicide rates than those with the death penalty, although such crude comparisons should not be taken seriously. The question of whether or not a state has capital punishment will not be the only factor influencing crime rates, by any means. At the same time, however, the *Times'* findings challenge the simplistic view that capital punishment is some kind of "magic cure" that is enough to prevent criminals from committing murder.

Statistics for the murder of police officers make sobering reading for promoters of capital punishment: those regions that use the death penalty the least seem to be the safest for police officers. In the South, which in 2000 accounted for 90 percent of all U.S. executions, 292 law enforcement officers were killed in the line of duty between 1989 and 1998. By comparison, the Northeast, the region with the fewest executions, saw only 80 officers murdered over that same period. A poll of police chiefs held in 1995 found them skeptical as to the deterrent value of the death penalty: 67 percent did not believe it did anything significant to reduce homicides.

MORE STATISTICS

But to talk of states that either do or do not have the death penalty is simplistic in itself. Wide variations are found in the extent to which those states that do have capital punishment actually use it. In 2000, for example, 85 prisoners were executed in 14 states: 40 in Texas; 11 in Oklahoma; 8 in

MAIN METHODS USED BY STATE

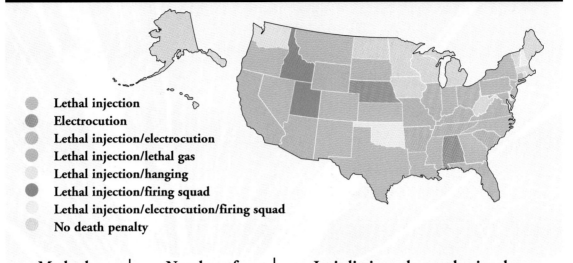

- ● Lethal injection
- ● Electrocution
- ● Lethal injection/electrocution
- ● Lethal injection/lethal gas
- ● Lethal injection/hanging
- ● Lethal injection/firing squad
- ● Lethal injection/electrocution/firing squad
- ● No death penalty

Method	Number of executions since 1976	Jurisdictions that authorize these methods of execution
Lethal injection	618	Alabama, Arizona, Arkansas, California, Colorado, Connecticut, Delaware, Florida, Georgia, Idaho, Illinois, Indiana, Kansas, Kentucky, Louisiana, Maryland, Mississippi, Missouri, Montana, Nevada, New Hampshire, New Jersey, New Mexico, New York, North Carolina, Ohio, Oklahoma, Oregon, Pennsylvania, South Carolina, South Dakota, Tennessee, Texas, Utah, Virginia, Washington, Wyoming, U.S. military, U.S. government
Electrocution	150	Alabama, Arkansas, Florida, Illinois, Kentucky, Nebraska, Oklahoma, South Carolina, Tennessee, Virginia
Gas chamber	11	Arizona, California, Maryland, Missouri, Wyoming
Hanging	3	Delaware, New Hampshire, Washington
Firing squad	2	Idaho, Oklahoma, Utah

The gas chamber at California's San Quentin Prison can, if necessary, cope with two executions at once. Normally, though, executions are conducted singly, with seat B being used in preference, being more accessible to the stethoscope that monitors heartbeats.

Virginia; 6 in Florida; 5 in Missouri; 4 in Alabama; 3 in Arizona; 2 in Arkansas, and one each in Delaware, Louisiana, North Carolina, South Carolina, Tennessee, and California.

All those executed had been found guilty of murder. In theory, the death

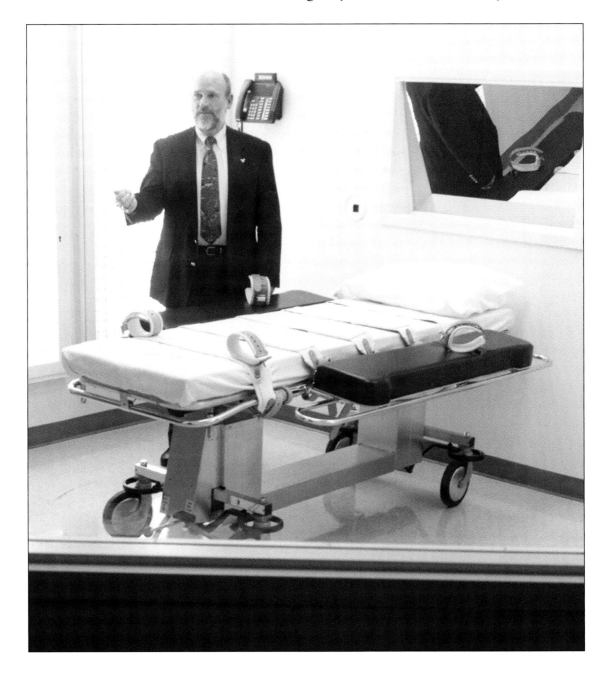

Warden David R. McKune conducts reporters around the execution suite at Kansas' Lansing Correctional Facility, 2001: the greatest care has been taken to make modern executions as humane as possible.

THE NOVELIST'S SONG

"You commit a murder Monday and commit a murder Tuesday. I wasn't waiting for Wednesday to come around." So said Brenda Nicol of Provo, Utah, before turning in her cousin Gary Gilmore (pictured), whom she had looked after in her home while he was out on parole from an armed-robbery sentence in the summer of 1976. Gilmore had indeed committed two murder-robberies in two days. The Utah court had little alternative but to order his execution. Yet, with the death penalty only just reintroduced in the wake of *Gregg v. Georgia*, there is little doubt that the condemned man could have spun out his time on Death Row with a series of appeals. Gilmore, however, refused to play what he saw as a legalistic game.

The desperate courage of this criminal struck some kind of chord with writer Norman Mailer, although he was impressed as well with the integrity of Brenda Nicol. Begun just after Gilmore's death, Mailer's famous book *The Executioner's Song* (1979) explores many of the complex ethical issues caused by the system as it stands, and the self-destructive victory Gilmore strove so hard to win by his dogged refusal to "play ball."

Tracy Housel's execution in Georgia, 2002, gave rise to trans-Atlantic tensions on account of his U.S.–British dual citizenship. The effect on public opinion was muted, though: while Britain did away with the death penalty decades ago, many ordinary people clearly regret its abolition.

penalty applies to other crimes, such as treason (betrayal of the nation), espionage (spying), aircraft hijacking resulting in death, or large-scale drug trafficking. In practice, such cases have been few and far between. Homicide has generally not been deemed sufficient in itself to warrant the imposition of the death penalty; it has to be aggravated by additional factors, which may vary from state to state. Generally, however, they include clear evidence of prior intent, a strong element of deliberate sexual violence—especially toward a child—or the commission of the murder in the course of some other major crime, such as political terrorism, drug smuggling, or kidnapping.

Of the 85 individuals executed in 2000, the overwhelming majority was men (only two were women), and the total masks another statistic, which some critics have found more sinister. While over half those executed (49) were white, 35 were African Americans, and one was of Native American origin.

The figure for African Americans is worryingly high for a group comprising only 12.9 percent of the U.S. population. Does it make it better or worse that this disproportion is dwarfed by the ratio of African Americans to white Americans in the ordinary

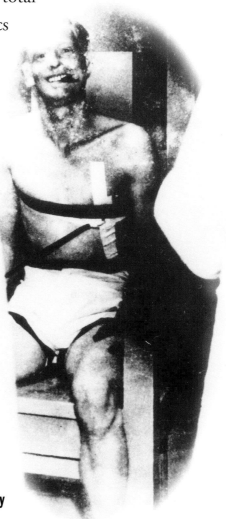

Convicted of a brutal murder, 23-year-old Jack Sullivan went to his death with a smile and a cigar, wisecracking even as he was strapped down in his seat in the gas chamber of Florence, Arizona, on May 25, 1936.

prison population? A problem rooted in a long and often bitter history of prejudice and exploitation, race remains a difficulty in just about every area of American life today. It would be naïve to suggest that the prejudices of centuries have been abolished. Yet, while it is tragically true that far too many African Americans are trapped in a desperate urban underclass, from which our more violent criminals tend to be drawn, there is no persuasive evidence of systematic "institutional racism" where capital punishment is concerned.

HOW THE DEATH PENALTY IS ADMINISTERED

Capital punishment has come a long way from the days of the rowdy "hanging fair." Today's executions are conducted with the utmost care and solemnity. For historical reasons, different states use different methods of execution, but minimizing suffering is always given high importance.

In the latter part of the 19th century, growing **humanitarian** concern came together with a general climate of technological progress to produce a major push to find a more "modern" method of execution. At a time when the wonders of electricity seemed to be transforming every other area of life, what could be more natural than that it should change capital punishment, too? Genuine humanitarian excitement greeted the first use of the electric chair, in New York in 1890, for the execution of ax murderer William Kemmler. "We live in a higher civilization from this day on," was one witness' report. "The man never suffered a bit of pain," claimed executioner's assistant George Fell. There seems to have been a certain amount of wishful thinking in both remarks. In fact, the current failed to kill Kemmler at the first attempt, so the chair had to be charged up again and the whole process repeated.

The first self-consciously "modern" method of execution, the electric chair was progressively improved as time went on. It is still among the most widely used methods of execution in the United States. Although the precise details vary from state to state, there are typically three executioners.

The heavy, airtight door of today's Arizona gas chamber, a more reliable and humane means of execution than it was in Jack Sullivan's day. Even so, it has gradually been replaced by lethal injection in the majority of cases.

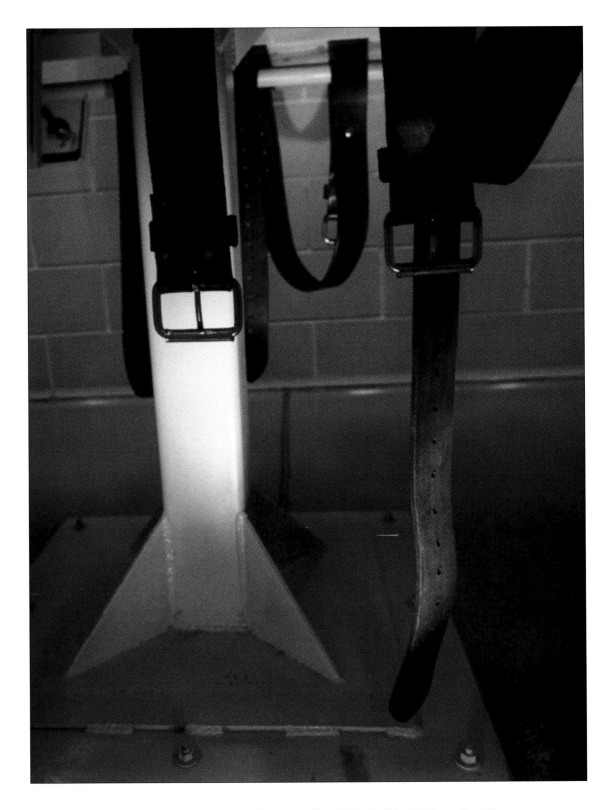

Buckled straps hang loosely down from the execution table in "Death House" at Florence, Arizona: the straps are necessary in order to hold a prisoner down while the lethal injection is administered.

Each throws a switch, but only one will be operating a "live" circuit. Which switch is the live one will not be known to the team, so no one member will have to feel solely responsible afterward. It is easy to forget that considerable emotional turmoil may be involved for the person charged by authorities with the taking of another's life, and measures like this minimize that trauma. This is why, in those states where execution by firing squad is used, one marksman will traditionally have a blank round in his magazine, so that no marksman will know for certain that he has been responsible for the prisoner's death.

CYANIDE AND LETHAL INJECTION

The first attempts to use cyanide gas as a means of execution in 1924 also met with practical difficulties. Attempts by prison authorities in Nevada to introduce it to the cell of murderer Gee Jon while he was sleeping proved unsuccessful, so an airtight gas chamber had to be constructed. As used currently in several states, the standard gas chamber is made of glass and steel, with an open pan beneath the prisoner's chair. Once the prisoner has been strapped in and the chamber sealed, hydrochloric acid is piped into the pan, after which potassium cyanide or sodium cyanide is dropped into the acid by mechanical means. The two compounds react to produce highly poisonous hydrocyanic gas, which causes unconsciousness in seconds, and death itself in a matter of minutes. As with other methods, a number of executioners may be involved and "dummy" equipment used, so that nobody knows for sure which one of them has actually brought about the prisoner's death.

A similar system may be used in injecting drugs into the intravenous tubes that deliver the "lethal injection," which is now the most widespread form of execution in the United States today. The condemned prisoner having been connected to a drip, three different drugs are usually administered in sequence, beginning with the general anesthetic sodium thiopental. Given at a dosage many times higher than that used in surgical

In March 2001, campaigners in Austin, Texas, stand at the entrance to Governor George W. Bush's mansion to protest the execution of Death Row inmate Odell Barnes.

operations, this drug itself may be enough to inflict death. It certainly ensures that the "patient" feels no pain as a paralyzing agent, pancuronium bromide, is introduced to prevent further breathing. Finally, potassium chloride is given: this causes shutdown in the electrical signaling needed if the heart is to remain operational; the result is immediate cardiac arrest.

Even lethal injection may have its drawbacks, however; for example, if the prisoner has had a history of heavy intravenous drug use, it can be hard to find a suitable vein. The perfect, foolproof system of execution has yet to be found. For this reason, some states have stuck with the traditionally tried-and-tested practice of hanging, believing it to be as effective and humane, on balance, as any other method since devised. In general, however, prisoners in these states will be offered the choice of death by another method (usually lethal injection). In fact, many states offer some degree of choice to all those prisoners condemned to death.

Even in those states most apparently committed to the use of the death penalty, strong "anti" organizations have emerged: here, protestors march in force outside the state capitol building in Austin, Texas. Texas has one of the most active death penalty policies in the United States.

The Death Penalty Worldwide

The United States is one of comparatively few countries that now has the death penalty on its statute books, a situation which has exposed it to some criticism. Not that we should necessarily let the opinions of others govern our actions; every nation has to follow the path that seems appropriate to it given the circumstances.

However, no one in the world was surprised by the effective abolition of capital punishment by the *Furman v. Georgia* Supreme Court decision of 1972. This move simply seemed to bring the United States into line with the vast majority of its Western allies. For many onlookers, Europeans especially, the United States' move was the culmination of two centuries' reform, which had seen capital punishment disappearing by degrees from all the major countries of the developed world.

Make no mistake: in taking steps to reintroduce the death penalty four years later, the United States was turning its back on the crowd, favoring its own independent conscience over the international consensus. Americans will not be cowed by the disapproval of overseas governments. In fact, they may take comfort from the abundant evidence that, in many of those countries where capital punishment is no longer used, there is strong public support for its reintroduction.

Left: The guillotine has become the most immediately recognizable symbol of the French Revolution and the painting shows a typical execution scene during the period infamously known as the "Reign of Terror," when members of the French aristocracy were beheaded one after another: few now realize that the guillotine was originally introduced as a humanitarian reform.

DYING OUT?

That same spirit of the Enlightenment that had done so much to form the thinking of Americans such as Benjamin Franklin and Thomas Jefferson influenced leaders in many other parts of the world as well. Ironically, its effects had been felt first of all, not where popular movements had agitated for it, but where strong monarchs had imposed it of their own free will. In what had then long been regarded as the most backward country in Europe—Russia—the Empress Elizabeth abolished the death penalty by royal decree in 1744. Prussian strongman Frederick the Great (1712–1786) followed suit a few years later. Joseph II of Austria (1741–1790) concluded the reforms of his late mother, the Empress Maria Theresa (1717–1780) by ending

Today, no more than a small, central-European nation, Austria was once the heart of a mighty empire: Joseph II's renunciation of the death penalty thus had an impact far and wide across 18th-century Europe and beyond.

Five revolutionaries are put to death in St. Petersburg in 1881, the presence of the priests not disguising the cruelty of the proceedings. The last decades of czarist rule saw Russia spiral into judicial savagery, as terrorist outrages met with vicious reprisals from the authorities.

capital punishment throughout what had once been the Holy Roman Empire. By the beginning of the 20th century, the death penalty had fallen into disuse across much of Europe (although it would not actually be abolished in Italy until 1994).

Simón Bolívar, and the other great 19th-century liberators of Latin America, also looked to the ideas of the Enlightenment as the inspiration in their nationalist programs. The republics they created represented these values, in however flawed a form. Countries like Venezuela and Ecuador, for instance, were leaders in abolishing the death penalty.

There were, however, backward steps as well. Struggling against revolutionaries, the late czars of Russia had little time for maintaining Elizabeth's high-minded reforms. And there were also, inevitably, **hypocrisies**. When the Communist Bolsheviks succeeded in supplanting the czars in 1917, one of their first acts was the abolition of capital punishment. Execution was, however, to be a predominant theme of the next few decades, when the Soviet state killed criminals, actual and political, by the thousands.

THE BLOODY CODE

Britain, home of the "Bloody Code," and as skeptical about Enlightenment ideas as about other things French, had long held out against the abolitionist tide that had been sweeping Europe. Even so, the number of crimes punishable by death dropped significantly in the course of the 19th century, while through the 20th century, the number of executions continued to fall.

As in the United States, all it took was for a single sensational case to make an enormous difference to how people felt. The case of Craig and Bentley in 1952, for example, caused great concern. Chris Craig, aged 16, and Derek Bentley, aged 19, broke into a South London warehouse. When cornered on the roof by police officers, Craig produced a gun and fired, apparently killing Constable Sydney Miles. There was no suggestion that the mentally backward Bentley had fired the fatal shot, or even been armed, and he had already been arrested when the offense took place. However, Craig was too young to hang, and Bentley had been his willing partner in a "joint venture." Accordingly, he was convicted of murder and executed.

Evidence would emerge much later to suggest that the "murdered" officer had fallen to "friendly fire" from police marksmen, and Bentley's "confession" looked highly dubious, his interrogators having forged his semiliterate signature six times. Yet many people felt from the first that the wretched Bentley had been made a **scapegoat** and had died the victim of a cruel and vindictive legal system.

"Debtors' Door," as it was commonly known, in London's Newgate Prison, was, for many hundreds of prisoners, an exit from life: it was through here that the condemned man or woman was led to the scaffold.

Guilty though she plainly was, Ruth Ellis was seen as a martyr by the British public: her execution helped advance the cause of abolition in that country. Advocates and enemies of capital punishment alike have had cause to rue the fickleness of public opinion.

A TALE OF TWO WOMEN

Ruth Ellis has her place in **penal** history as the last woman to have been hanged in Britain, in 1955. The manageress of a London nightclub, she had murdered her lover, David Blakely. Hers was undoubtedly a sad story. Blakely had been faithless, and on occasion, violent. He had cruelly stoked up Ellis' jealousy and laughed at her anguish. Yet she herself did not dispute that she had shot him dead or that she had come armed to seek him out and shoot him. Indeed, she had borrowed the revolver from a friend for this specific purpose. However, her death sentence threw Britain's press and public into turmoil. Thousands signed petitions for her **reprieve** (although there were no grounds), and her execution lent enormous impetus to the campaign for the abolition of capital punishment.

That was duly passed by Parliament a decade later, but barely was the ink on the statute dry than the country was shocked by news from northern England of the "Moors Murders." A young couple, Ian Brady and Myra Hindley, were found to have abducted and murdered a number of children on the moors (wild wasteland) in the hills above Manchester. The victims had been raped and tortured before they were killed, it seemed. In at least one case, their murderers had taped the proceedings.

Brady had clearly been the dominant partner, but there could be no doubt whatsoever of Hindley's close support. In particular, it was she who approached the children to gain their confidence prior to their kidnappings. With her brassy bleached-blonde hairdo, she was reminiscent of Ruth Ellis in looks, but Myra Hindley was destined to evoke a very different public reaction. For four decades, she has arguably been Britain's best-known icon of evil, and people's nostalgia for the days of the death penalty can be said to have begun with her. What makes people particularly uncomfortable is the possibility that someone guilty of such a crime should ever be released.

After Britain's abolition of the death penalty in 1965, most of the Commonwealth followed suit: the countries of the former British Empire

Supporters of the human-rights group Amnesty International in Hong Kong have protested outside the territory's Chinese and American missions, voicing their objections to the use of capital punishment by both the dictatorship and the democracy.

AN EXECUTION IN CHINA

Pro-democracy campaigner Harry Wu has described the day in 1983 when he stepped out into the streets of Zhengzhou, Henan Province, to find the place deserted. "In a city of two million," he recalled, "it seemed that all work and school had come to a stop. I estimated later that close to half the city's population must have left their jobs and classrooms." Soon, he came upon the crowd, lining a main route through town, he wrote, then, "45 flatbed trucks, one after another, rolled by…at the front of each truck bed, just behind the cab, stood a condemned man bound with heavy rope. The rope ran in an X across his chest and around to his back, holding in place a tall narrow sign. On the top half of each sign was an accusation: 'Thief,' 'Murderer,' 'Rapist.' On the bottom half was the name of the accused, marked through with a large red X."

The procession threaded its way through the town to wind up at a field in the outskirts. There, the prisoners were forced to kneel beside shallow graves before each was killed with a single shot to the back of the head.

still had close cultural and political ties. In Africa, Angola and Mozambique had abolished capital punishment, along with their Portuguese "mother country," in the middle of the 19th century. Although strained by the ravages of civil war, the reform would at least, in principle, survive the transition to independence.

AMERICA ARRAIGNED

Opponents of the death penalty point out that its use places the United States in some strange international company, with **Communist** countries

Capital punishment is not always administered with the scrupulousness with which it is applied in America. Human-rights groups claim that these alleged "mutineers" in Guinea, West Africa, are being subjected to what amounts to a crude show-trial.

like China and North Korea, as well as with Islamic extremist nations of one sort or another, like Libya, Iraq, and Iran. Public beheadings remain a feature of life in modern Saudi Arabia. However, executions ordered by Iran's religious rulers have been met with an increasingly furious public backlash in recent years, with ordinary Iranians unprepared to accept the killing of their men and women, often for offenses of sexual morality, which they do not recognize as actual crimes.

In 1998, in the city of Marshad, 5,000 protestors forced the authorities to call off the execution of one woman. Three years later, police fired tear gas at a similar demonstration in the capital, Tehran.

How far we should allow ourselves to be shamed by association with such states is in any case extremely doubtful. Capital punishment is entirely different in both underlying philosophy and actual administration here. Use of the death penalty is just one point of comparison between otherwise dissimilar cultures: the United States is entirely unlike these countries in so many other ways. And in addition to the few "rogue states," many countries still have capital punishment on their statute books, even if it is never used.

It remains true, however, that the United States is isolated in the community of advanced industrialized countries, and European writers and politicians have frequently made accusations of "barbarism." Yet Americans might reasonably wonder whether such fastidious disdain does not owe more to cultural snobbishness than genuine humanitarianism: the elite of the Old World has never felt comfortable acknowledging the achievements of the United States. For a generation, soaring levels of violent crime allowed European commentators to present the United States as a continuation of the "Wild West," with capital punishment caricatured as a form of "cowboy law."

More recently, however, the rate of violent crime in America has dropped sharply, while European rates have risen to meet them. And there is evidence that many ordinary people actually want a return to the death penalty. By no means do all Europeans support the use of the death penalty,

A NATIONAL SPORT?

The staging of public executions in Kabul's main soccer stadium was one of many barbaric features of life in Afghanistan under the ultra-Islamic rule of the Taliban. Thousands were compelled to watch as men and women were shot for adultery or other public morality "crimes" or offenses against the Islamic state. Generally speaking, the executions themselves were only the climax of a carefully directed theater of cruelty. As a prelude, teenage lovers might be publicly married before being whipped with 100 lashes each. Decent Muslims around the world were shocked at what they saw as the Prophet's teachings being manipulated in order to support a repressive regime.

any more than do all Americans, but poll after poll has suggested strong reservations about present policy.

In both France and Italy, around 50 percent of the population would support its reintroduction. The gap between elite and electorate is shown most starkly in Britain, where several attempts to reinstate capital punishment have been overwhelmingly rejected in the country's Parliament, despite levels of popular support running at between 66 and 75 percent over many years.

Should the United States take any notice at all of international opinion? The answer has to be "Yes, but not too much." Any teenager understands the dangers of giving in too easily to "peer pressure": we should not even think of changing our system of justice merely as a means of "fitting in" with those countries we see as our natural friends. Yet that is not to say that we have no responsibilities whatsoever to the world at large.

The eyes of all, we have to be aware, are on the world's most powerful and influential nation: others look to us for leadership in the way they

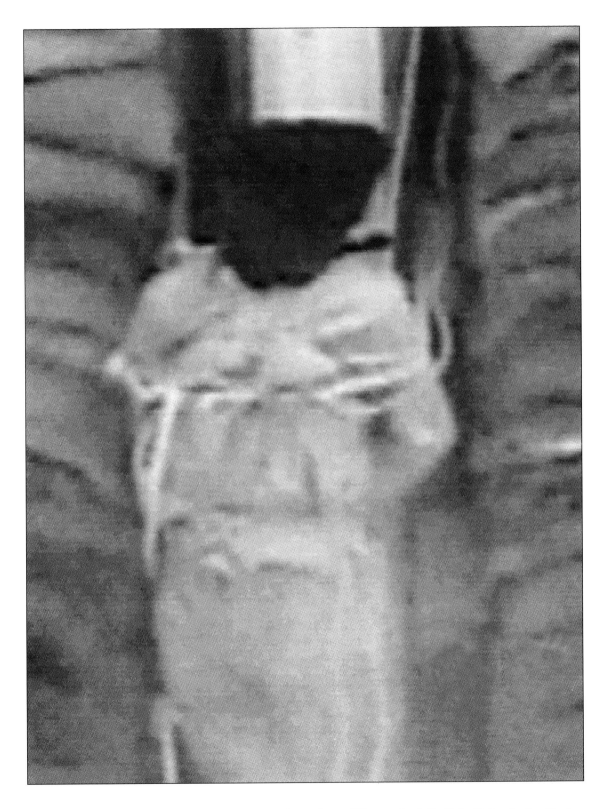

Majdi Mikkawi was killed by firing squad on the orders of Yasser Arafat's Palestinian Authority for his alleged collaboration with Israeli forces. His death was chillingly captured in this amateur video of January 13, 2001.

Kerry Max Cook spent over 17 years on Death Row in Huntsville, Texas, before proved innocent and freed in 1999. Now he travels all over the world campaigning against capital punishment: here, he speaks at a European Union-organized conference in Strasbourg, France.

A demonstrator in Vienna, Austria, sports a noose around his neck as he holds up photos of the captured Kurdish separatist leader Abdulla Ocalan, condemned to hang by the Turkish authorities, who claim he is a terrorist.

conduct their own affairs. Repressive rulers may even seek to justify their cruelties by reference to the existence of the death penalty in the world's greatest democracy: the comparison may be ridiculous, but we can still expect it to be made.

Like any individual person, a country like America can only examine its collective conscience, considering its duty both to its own citizens and to the wider world-community in which it lives.

Death Row

The people whose responsibility it is to administer the death penalty in America—politicians, judges, lawyers, and prison authorities—are only too conscious of the heavy moral burden they have assumed. The prosecutor who calls on the court to impose the death penalty, the judges and juries whose decision it is: all these act in the awareness that their place in the judicial process has given them extraordinary powers over life and death.

The prison officials and staff who have the task of carrying out the execution realize that only the gravest of offenses could conceivably justify the taking of another life. Hence, the extensive and elaborate system of safeguards and appeal procedures that allow the course of justice to be halted at any point, if even the slightest doubt should arise that justice is not being done. However, so complicated a system takes a great deal of time; it may take years to exhaust the possibilities of appeal, throughout which period the prisoner resides on what is popularly referred to as "Death Row." This is both a physical location in the jail, set apart from the rest, and a separate psychological place between life and death, another world, with its own customs, its own ways.

In the year 2000, 3,593 people were living under the sentence of death in U.S. prisons. Although mostly men, there were 54 women on Death Row. The statistical "over-representation" of African Americans among those executed (discussed earlier) was matched by the number living under death sentence, which at 1,535, did not fall that far short of the figure for

Left: An Austin, Texas, demonstrator has a Scripture lesson for then-presidential candidate George W. Bush—the Bible's line on capital punishment is actually less clear-cut than the Fifth Commandment makes it seem.

Texas prisoner Genaro Comacho, Jr. looks out from the semi-darkness of his Death Row cell. Inmates will typically spend years at a time here in what amounts to another world before going on to face their final earthly punishment.

Death Row is its own society, with its own culture and its own mythology: Texas inmate Jamaar Arnold has gained notoriety as "the meanest man on Death Row."

whites (1,990). Also listed were 29 Native Americans, 27 Asians, and another 12 described as being "of unknown race." Hardened criminals, for the most part, almost two out of three had prior convictions for major offenses. One in 12, indeed, had committed homicides before. The average age at the time of arrest was 28, although a small minority (two percent) had been apprehended at age 17 or younger.

LIFE ON DEATH ROW

At the beginning of 2002, the state of Colorado had six inmates on Death Row: all male, their ages ranged from 26 to 46. In his forties, Frank Rodriguez had been convicted in 1987 of the rape and murder of a Denver

LAWS UNTO THEMSELVES

The old Soviet ways seem to be dying hard in Russia and Ukraine, both of which are currently under threat of expulsion from the Council of Europe. Although nominally committed to an impressive-sounding system of checks and balances, evidence has been piling up in recent years that the authorities have been quietly dispensing with jury trials and even carrying out executions in secret, making a mockery of those provisions, which, in theory, exist for appeal.

Though appalled, international observers have hardly been surprised at these revelations. Under both the czarist and Communist regimes, Russia and Ukraine were highly authoritarian, even militaristic, societies. Neither legal system had any tradition of allowing the judgments of ranking officials to be questioned, and execution has always been by firing squad, in the military manner.

bookkeeper. A decade and a half on Death Row may sound like a long time, but Rodriguez's case is by no means unusual. Across the U.S., the average gap between conviction and execution is around eight years.

In a complicated case, or where (as with Colorado) the state has a tradition of reluctance to execute, longer stays on Death Row are quite routine. No other Colorado inmate had been there as long as Rodriguez, however. Next in seniority came Robert Harlan (born July 7, 1964), convicted in 1995 of the murder of a casino waitress and the attempted murder of another woman who had come to her aid. The youngest and the oldest inmates, as it happens, had both been convicted as recently as 2000: George Woldt (born November 8, 1976), for the murder of a female college student, and William C. Neal, who carried out the execution-style murder

Every inmate has his hard-luck story, but some are undoubtedly more colorful than others: Sayed Rabani (above) claims to be a Bangladeshi diplomat being held as a political prisoner by the state of Texas.

Only when he has been safely installed in his cell may New Mexico inmate Timothy Allen have his handcuffs removed: for obvious reasons, any movement within the prison has to be conducted with the utmost security.

Death Row was designed with security in mind, not beauty or a welcoming atmosphere: here, a guard walks through "A" Pod, "F" section of the Polunsky Unit, Livingston, Texas. Death Row security personnel have to be ready for any eventuality from these highly dangerous prisoners.

of three women in Jefferson County.

Death Row is a separate facility at the Colorado State Penitentiary. Inmates remain there, in single cells, until their appointed "warrant week"—the week of execution—when they are moved to a separate holding cell in the execution suite. For the sake of security, these dangerous inmates are locked down in their cells for 23 hours a day, with an hour allowed for exercise and showering. If they have to be moved for any reason, it will be with "full restraint" (in cuffs and ankle irons) and under the supervision of at least two prison guards.

For security's sake, all essential services are brought to the inmates in their cells. This includes any medication, educational materials, library

A VOICE FROM DEATH ROW

The following is an entry from the journal of David Paul Hammer, awaiting execution at Terre Haute, Indiana, for Wednesday, December 12, 2001.

"After hours of restless sleep where I tossed and turned, I decided to get up. The sun won't be up for hours, and the silence of the Row is creepy. The place has a dead feel to it. The only sounds I've heard were those of the officers doing their count, flashlights beamed into cells of sleeping convicts, nothing appears amiss, so they move on, and then out of hearing range. The only noise to alert me to their presence is the steady jingling of keys as they climb the stairs or walk the tiers. All is quiet now.

"I stood at my cell window, watching nothing but the dead of night. Only a few feet from this unit is the top of the building housing the prison commissary. The roof of that structure is covered with stones the size of golf balls, all shapes and colors. In the pale yellow glow cast by the security light, these rocks seem to glow. Razor-sharp wire in coils are affixed atop the roof's edge to prevent anyone from climbing onto the building...Alone in the early morning hours, my mind screams. There's no escape from the reminders that surround me. Prison...my home."

A wary guard looks on as Arkansas inmate Eugene Wallace Perry is prepared for a visit: outside his cell, the prisoner's every move is carefully controlled. Many Death Row inmates are highly dangerous people.

More than 400 prisoners are held in Texas' Death Row facility, the Polunsky Unit at Livingston, 75 miles northeast of Houston. Here their accommodation is spartan but serviceable and, more importantly, it is secure.

books, and food. Visits (two and a half hours a week) with family, lawyers, or media are held in a designated area within the facility, where no physical contact with outsiders can be made. Three times a day—and on extra occasions as necessary—a formal count is held to ensure that all inmates are safely in their cells. The Colorado system allows inmates a TV, radio, newspapers, magazines, and two books at a time in their cells. The days can pass extraordinarily slowly on Death Row. Access is allowed to the facility's own general and law libraries and to movies shown regularly by the authorities. There are three meals a day. Lower-category prisoners in another part of the penitentiary do cooking, and prison officers bring them across to Death Row.

WARRANT WEEK

When warrant week comes, the routine shifts up a notch, and extra visiting privileges are routinely granted at this time. On the day of the execution, after meeting with an approved spiritual adviser in preparation for death, the inmate will have his traditional choice of "last meal" at the normal time. He may choose anything the prison's food service department has in stock at the time. Ninety minutes before execution, he is allowed to shower and change into a clean green uniform: pants, button-up shirt, socks, and shoes. Thirty minutes before the appointed time, he is taken from his cell by a specialized "strap down" team, who will ensure that he is properly fastened down on the execution bed. With around 20 minutes still to run, the IV team will insert the drips for the lethal injection: ample time must be allowed for what can, on occasion, be a tricky procedure.

After the warden has read the execution warrant to the prisoner— usually with around eight minutes still remaining—selected witnesses will be ushered into an adjacent observation room. These will generally include close family members, the prosecuting and defense attorneys, and a member of the law enforcement agency who first brought the prisoner to justice, in addition to approved representatives of the media.

Up until this point, the execution chamber can be contacted by telephone, just in case a reprieve or stay of execution should come through. Now, however, it is deemed that the proceedings have reached the point of no return and the warden formally disconnects the telephone. The order is then given for the lethal injection to be administered. Two minutes later,

There may be precious little space in the standard Death Row cell, but the prisoner still has some scope for making himself at home: the wall of inmate Jamaar Arnold's is festooned with his various papers.

THE ROAD TO DEATH ROW

Records held by the Texas Department of Criminal Justice give a sense of the life of Jeffery Tucker, executed November 14, 2001, for the July 1988 shooting of the owner of a truck he planned to steal. This had, however, been only the last in a steadily escalating series of offenses, committed in the course of the 1980s, which had seen Tucker progress from minor theft and marijuana smoking to forgery and aggravated assault. Before being arrested outside Santa Rosa, New Mexico, he had committed another armed robbery.

There is no reason to suppose that—had he remained free—his first murder would have been his last. Having exhausted all his appeals, Tucker seems to have met death in a philosophical spirit. The approach of eternity certainly seems not to have affected his appetite appreciably. For his last meal, his order was as follows: "6 pieces of fried chicken, potato salad with mustard, macaroni and cheese, 8 cinnamon rolls, 1 pint of vanilla ice cream, pitcher of milk, and ketchup."

the coroner is asked to enter the chamber to pronounce death and record the time. Once this has been done, the witnesses are escorted to the lobby of the execution suite to sign the record of execution.

ESCAPING THE FINALITY

The death penalty is society's ultimate sanction, and it is never imposed lightly. An elaborate system of checks and balances exists to prevent the possibility of error or injustice. There are two separate systems of appeals, state and federal. In fact, the former arguably constitutes two systems in itself, since the prisoner can first appeal the sentence directly all the way up to the United States Supreme Court, then if that fails, start all over again, appealing particular technical details of his trial to ever-higher levels.

If sympathetic to the arguments made on a prisoner's behalf, the state governor may intervene in the process, in some cases ordering a "commutation of sentence" (a reduction from death penalty to life imprisonment) or even a complete **pardon**. More often, he or she will issue a temporary "reprieve" or "stay of execution" to allow a particular point of law or investigative angle to be explored.

For many prisoners, the research and work involved in pursuing the possible legal avenues can become an occupation, offering a sense of purpose in life (and, in some cases, the start of an academic interest). For society at large, all these procedures are a mixed blessing. At best, they introduce bureaucratic complexity and lengthy delays to the administration of the death penalty. At worst, they open the system up to cynical exploitation, although this is generally regarded as a price worth paying. Better the abuse of such safeguards by the guilty than that an unwarranted execution should take place and a man or woman be killed unjustly.

And there are precedents for the system getting it wrong. In 1996, Dennis Williams walked free from a Chicago court after 18 years on Death Row, one of three men convicted—but now cleared by DNA evidence—of a terrible double murder.

The proof of the pudding—or, rather, the steak—and a triumphant vindication of our system of appeals, as Roberto Miranda happily sits down to celebrate his release after 14 years on Florida's Death Row.

GLOSSARY

Abolition: the act of ending the observance or effect of something, especially relating to laws

Bifurcated: divided into two branches or parts

"Bloody Code": popular expression for the list of offenses punishable by death in Britain. It grew in length through the 18th century

Communism: political creed that calls for all private property to be taken into the possession of the state

Democracy: a community or country in which the people control their government

Exile: the state or period of forced absence from one's country or home

Humane: showing compassion for other human beings or animals

Humanitarian: concerned to protect the interests of humanity

Hypocrisy: a pretending to be what one is not or to believe what one does not

Infallibility: the impossibility of making a mistake

Intellectual: a person devoted to study and thought, especially about profound or philosophical issues

Mandatory: containing or constituting a command; obligatory

Miscreant: one who behaves criminally or viciously

Pardon: decision of a state governor (or, in the case of a "presidential pardon," the president of the United States) to free a prisoner from all legal consequences of a particular offense

Penal: relating to penalties or prisons

Reprieve or **stay of execution**: calling of a temporary halt to an execution to allow all legal avenues to be explored

Satirical: relating to the use of wit, irony, or sarcasm to expose human vices and follies

Scapegoat: someone who wrongfully takes the blame for others

Shariya: the system of law ordained for Muslims by Islamic tradition

CHRONOLOGY

1775 B.C.:	Babylonian "Code of Hammurabi," the first known legal system.
800:	Early Romans throw traitors to their deaths from the Tarpeian Rock.
100:	Their empire expanding into the Middle East, the Romans are influenced by local practices, such as crucifixion.
A.D. 1608:	Captain George Kendall is executed; this is the first recorded case in the American colonies.
1632:	Jane Champion is executed; she is the first woman known to have been executed in the American colonies.
1744:	Empress Elizabeth abolishes the death penalty in Russia.
1764:	Cesare Beccaria's *Essay on Crimes and Punishments* is published; it was considered the classic expression of Enlightenment thinking on this issue.
1834:	Pennsylvania moves executions inside correctional facilities.
1845:	The American Society for the Abolition of Capital Punishment is established.
1859:	John Brown is executed at Charlestown, West Virginia.
1892:	Newton Curtis introduces his (unsuccessful) bill for complete abolition of capital punishment at a federal level.
1897:	"An Act to Reduce the Cases in Which the Death Penalty May be Inflicted" is passed by Congress.
1846:	Michigan abolishes the death penalty for all crimes except treason.
1890:	William Kemmler is the first person to die in the electric chair.
1924:	Nevada becomes the first state to use cyanide gas in executions; the refusal of a Chicago court to give the death sentence in the case of "Thrill Killers" Richard Loeb and Nathan Leopold, Jr. causes public outcry.

1927: The execution of Nicola Sacco and Bartolomeo Vanzetti causes another public outcry.

1958: *Trop v. Dulles* Supreme Court judgment acknowledges the possibility that standards of decency may change in a "maturing society."

1965: Hanging is abolished in Britain.

1972: *Furman v. Georgia* judgment effectively abolishes the death penalty in the U.S.

1976: *Gregg v. Georgia* effectively reinstates the death penalty.

1977: Gary Gilmore is executed by a Utah firing squad; Oklahoma becomes the first state to use lethal injection in executions.

1996: European Union makes complete abolition of capital punishment a condition of membership; for most member states, this means little more than the formal confirmation of existing laws.

FURTHER INFORMATION

Useful Web Sites

www.ojp.usdoj.gov/bjs/cp: For the best single source of information on capital punishment as currently applied in the United States.

www.usinfo.state.gov/topical/rights/hrpage/cp: For a wider overview of the history of capital punishment and the main moral, legal, and constitutional issues involved, see the State Department's informational briefing.

www.tdcj.tx.state.us, www.cdc.state.ca.us/issues/capital, and www.doc.state.co.us: For more specialized information of individual state justice departments, including the Texas Department of Criminal Justice, California, and Colorado.

www.howstuffworks.com: For interesting discussion of some actual methods of capital punishment.

Further Reading

Banner, Stuart. *The Death Penalty: An American History.* Cambridge, MA: Harvard University Press, 2002.

Bedau, Hugo Adam (ed.). *The Death Penalty in America: Current Controversies.* New York: Oxford University Press, 1998.

Sarat, Austin. *When the State Kills: Capital Punishment and the American Condition.* Princeton, NJ: Princeton University Press, 2001.

Solotaroff, Ivan. *The Last Face You'll Ever See: The Private Life of the American Death Penalty.* New York: HarperCollins, 2001.

About the Author

Michael Kerrigan was born in Liverpool, England, and educated at St. Edward's College, from where he won an Open Scholarship to University College, Oxford. He lived for a time in the United States, spending time first at Princeton, followed by a period working in publishing in New York. Since then he has been a freelance writer and journalist, with commissions across a wide range of subjects, but with a special interest in social policy and defense issues. Within this field, he has written on every region of the world.

His work has been published by leading international educational publishers, including the BBC, Dorling Kindersley, Time-Life, and Reader's Digest Books. His work as a journalist includes regular contributions to the *Times Literary Supplement*, London, as well as a weekly column in the *Scotsman* newspaper, Edinburgh, where he now lives with his wife and their two small children.

INDEX

T 58369